Animals that Work

Sue Barraclough

Raintree

Chicago, Illinois

Customer Service   888–454–2279

Visit our website at www.heinemannlibrary.com

Photo research by Ruth Blair and Kay Altwegg
Designed by Jo Hinton-Malivoire and bigtop design ltd
Printed and bound in China by South China Printing Company
12 11 10 09
10 9 8 7 6 5 4 3 2

Library of Congress Cataloging-in-Publication Data
Barraclough, Sue.
  Animals that work / Sue Barraclough.
     p. cm. -- (Animal worlds)
  Includes index.
  ISBN 1-4109-1897-1 (lib. bdg.) -- ISBN 1-4109-1902-1 (pbk.)
  ISBN 978-1-4109-1897-0 (lib. bdg.) -- ISBN 978-1-4109-1902-1 (pbk.)
  1. Working animals--Juvenile literature. I. Title. II. Series: Barraclough, Sue. Animal worlds.
SF172.B37 2005
636.088'6--dc22

                              2005006755
Acknowledgments
The author and publisher are grateful to the following for permission to reproduce copyright
material: Alamy/Charlie Barland p. 19; Alamy/Paul Wayne Wilson p. 11; Alamy/Shout p. 15;
Ardea London Ltd/John Daniels p. 8; Corbis/Dave Bartruff p. 20; Corbis/Jim Craigmyle p. 12;
Corbis/Kevin R. Morris p. 6; Corbis/Paul A. Souders p. 10; Corbis/Ron Sanford p. 18;
Corbis/Tim Graham p. 22; Getty Images/Photodisc p. 13; Harcourt Index p. 9; Jean Paul
Ferrero/Ardea London Ltd p. 18; Naturepl.com/Aflo p. 23; NHPA/Brian & Cherry Alexander
pp. 4, 5; NHPA/Danie Heuclin p. 15; NHPA/E Hanumantha Rao p. 7; NHPA/Martin Harvey p.
14; NHPA/Norburt Wu p. 21; NHPA/Steve Robinson p. 17; Rex Features p. 16.

Cover photograph reproduced with permission of photolibrary.com.

Some words are shown in bold, **like this**. You can find out
what they mean by looking in the glossary.

2

Contents

Animals that Work 4

Different Working Animals 6

Stables and Kennels 8

Food and Water 10

Animals at Work 12

Learning How 14

Special Jobs 16

Making Noises 18

Holidays 20

Caring and Cleaning 22

Glossary 24

Index 24

Animals that Work

Some animals help us do things. They are called working animals.

These dogs pull sleds across the snow.

Different working Animals

All kinds of animals can work.

Dogs run fast.
They can help
round up cattle.

Why do you think
this farmer rides the horse?

Strong animals help carry heavy loads.

This elephant uses its trunk to pick up logs.

Stables and Kennels

Working animals need somewhere to sleep that is warm and dry.

Horses live in **stables**.

Dogs live in **Kennels**.

Food and Water

All animals need to eat food to give them energy.

Horses like to eat hay.

Animals at Work

Animals help people in many ways.

Donkeys can help carry heavy loads.

Guide dogs help their owners by leading them around safely.

13

Learning How

Working animals have to learn how to do their jobs.

These elephants learn how to move huge logs.

This dog learns how to find people who are lost in the snow.

Special Jobs

Some animals have special jobs.

Police horses are big and strong. They carry police officers on **patrol**.

Dogs have a good sense of smell.
They use their noses to find things.

Making Noises

Working animals make all kinds of noises.

WOOF!

Guard dogs bark loudly.

Holidays

Working animals need time to relax and play.

These army horses are having a day out at the beach.

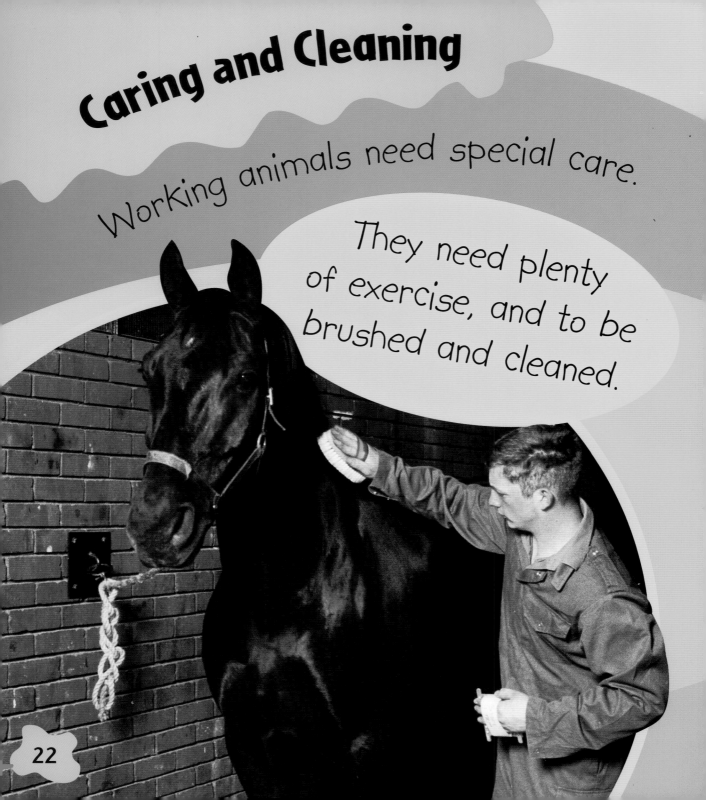

Caring and Cleaning

Working animals need special care.

They need plenty of exercise, and to be brushed and cleaned.

All animals need a place
to rest and sleep.

Glossary

Kennel place where dogs live

patrol travel along a certain path to watch for things

stable place where horses and cows live

Index

care 22

drink 11

farmer 6

food 10

guide dogs 13

noises 18

relax 20

sleep 8, 23

Notes for adults

Animal Worlds investigates a variety of animals by looking at their distinguishing features and characteristics and by exploring their different environments.

This series supports a young child's knowledge and understanding of their world. The books are designed to help children extend their vocabulary as they are introduced to new words. Words are used in context in each book to enable young children to gradually incorporate them into their own vocabulary.

Follow-up activities:

Encourage children to draw and record what they have learned about working animals, and to notice any differences or similarities when compared to other animals in the series.